Friends Forever!

Story by Rose Inserra
Illustrations by Alina Tysoe

Friends Forever!

Text: Rose Inserra
Series consultant: Annette Smith
Publishing editor: Simone Calderwood
Editors: Sarah Blood and Ted Carisbrooke
Project editor: Annabel Smith
Designer: Karen Mayo
Series designers: James Lowe and Karen Mayo
Illustrations: Alina Tysoe
Production controller: Erin Dowling
Reprint: Siew Han Ong

PM Guided Reading
Sapphire Level 30

Darwin Wong Goes to China
Friends Forever!
Explosive Volcanoes
Beware of the Mist
Space Technology in Space and on Earth
Riverboat Boy
Digging Up the Past
Unexplained Mysteries
Passing Through
They Fought for Justice

ISBN 978 0 17 037945 8

Cengage Learning Australia
Level 5 , 80 Dorcas Street
Southbank VIC 3006
Phone: 1300 790 853
Email: aust.nelsonprimary@cengage.com

For learning solutions, visit cengage.com.au

Printed in China by 1010 Printing International Ltd
12 23

Contents

Chapter 1	Cara and Sophie	5
Chapter 2	Liam	11
Chapter 3	Georgia	17
Chapter 4	Auditions	24
Chapter 5	An Unexpected Try-out	32
Chapter 6	The Announcement	38
Chapter 7	Some Unfortunate Events	42
Chapter 8	A Special Request	50
Chapter 9	Break a Leg!	57

Chapter 1

Cara and Sophie

"Just say you're feeling sick," Cara said. "It's not fair. You'll just get teased as usual."

Sophie looked miserably at her twin. "I know. I hate the way everyone laughs at me when I have to speak up in class."

Sophie couldn't help but feel sorry for herself. She remembered how speaking in front of people made her feel: her heart thumped and hammered in her chest, so loudly that she was sure people could hear it; the knot in her stomach made her feel sick; her hands were clammy; and when she tried to speak, her throat locked up and made it hard to even breathe.

Nothing came out – not a single sound. She tried and tried to let the words out but her voice remained trapped inside.

Then a small grunt or moan came from somewhere, followed by the dreaded stutter, and the horrible silence after each word.

The silence was just awful. Sophie could hear her classmates giggle, shuffle their feet and distract themselves so that they wouldn't have to hear her strain to get the words out.

"Stuttering Sophie" – that was what she had overheard someone call her.

Cara saw Sophie blinking back the tears.

"Don't worry, Sophie," she said reassuringly. "I'll distract the class. I'll drop my book accidentally or turn the volume up really loud on my laptop."

Sophie wanted to smile. She fought to keep herself from crying.

"Why does Mr Sol want to make me read my answer in front of everyone?" she said. "It's not fair. He knows I'm not like everyone else."

"Well, maybe Mr Sol wants you to become more confident when you speak. He doesn't like people being treated differently if they have … you know …" said Cara.

"Yeah, I know. Like me – if they have a stutter," replied Sophie, quietly. "Except what Mr Sol doesn't know is that I get teased and bullied about it. They're cunning, those bullies. They only tease and embarrass me when the teachers aren't around. And there are other kids who get bullied, too."

Cara nodded. "I know, but one day the bullies will slip up and get caught. Don't worry, Sophie. But for now, there's something you can do."

Cara held up a DVD of the movie *Aladdin*.

"I have no idea what you're talking about," Sophie said, confused.

"You could prove them all wrong by singing in the musical! I found out we're going to be performing *Aladdin: The Musical* for our end-of-year concert," replied Cara. "It's technically still a secret until tomorrow. I overheard Miss Golding telling Mr Sol this morning."

“I still don’t understand what that’s got to do with helping me talk in front of the class tomorrow, or avoiding getting teased at recess,” said Sophie, feeling frustrated. “You just don’t understand how I feel, Cara.”

Before Cara could say another word, Sophie ran out of the living room and into her bedroom, slamming the door behind her.

“Oh, you girls aren’t arguing again, are you?” called out their mum from the kitchen.

“No, Mum,” replied Cara. “Everything’s fine. Don’t worry about it.”

But Sophie and Cara’s mum did worry about it. She knew that Sophie had a difficult time at school. She would have to call Mr Sol again and ask if there had been any more incidents of bullying.

Sophie lay on her bed and listened to her favourite music. She must have drifted off to sleep, because when Mum knocked on her door to tell her it was time for dinner, Sophie remembered her strange dream.

She dreamt she was performing as Princess Jasmine from *Aladdin* at the end-of-year concert in front of the whole school.

She sang so beautifully that everyone clapped and cried out for more. What was amazing was that she sang alone – solo. And even more amazing – she didn't stutter.

Not one little bit.

Her voice sounded like magic.

She felt disappointed it was all a dream. *Of course it was only a dream. There's no such thing as magic,* she told herself, sadly.

Chapter 2

Liam

Liam was not excited about starting at a new school.

"It's going to be fine, Liam. They have a wonderful music program and some fun after-school activities – dancing, art, robotics, chess and lots of other things," said Liam's dad, trying to cheer him up.

"I'm still going to miss my friends," Liam grumbled.

"Come on, Liam. You know we wouldn't have moved here if we'd had another choice," said his mum. "But Dad's new job here means that we will be able to do so many things in the city that we couldn't do before, like go to museums, live concerts, sports matches, street festivals, the movies, shows, the beach … I can name so many things!" she continued cheerfully.

But Liam found it difficult to share his mum's enthusiasm.

He missed their old town, their house and the big backyard with chickens, the horse Freckles in the paddock next door that he was allowed to ride, his old school mates.

"You'll make new friends," said his dad. "Just be yourself. Be friendly and smile."

If only it could be that easy, thought Liam. *At least it's bigger than my old school, so maybe I'll find a friend on my first day.*

Liam's first day at his new city school made him nervous. It wasn't anything like his old school – it was huge! He was lost – all the buildings looked the same. He wished he hadn't told his mum and dad to leave him at the gate.

"Hey, you're new, aren't you?" said a voice behind him.

Liam turned around. Two girls had just walked across the schoolyard from the car drop-off area and were heading in the direction of the red brick building.

"Yeah, um … kind of," replied Liam, feeling embarrassed.

"My name's Cara and this is my sister, Sophie," said the girl. "We're in 6B. What about you?"

"I'm Liam and I'm in 6B, too," said Liam, feeling relieved that he had found at least two classmates and they seemed friendly.

The girls looked identical apart from their hairstyle. Sophie's hair was long and tied in a ponytail. Cara's hair was in a bob, and she had coloured clips to hold it back.

"Yes, you've guessed," said Cara, noticing Liam staring at both of them. "We're twins. And yeah, I'm the loud one."

Sophie gave her an annoyed look, and said a quiet “Hi”.

“You can come with us, Liam,” said Cara, pointing to the building. “We’re going to put our bags away first, and then we’ll take you to our classroom. You can sit at our table.”

Maybe things aren’t going to be so bad, thought Liam.

But by lunchtime, Liam discovered the terrible truth. This school was no different from his old school. Most of the boys tended to play sport, while the girls chatted together in groups.

Liam wasn't interested in sport – and that made him stand out as being different from the other boys.

"Hey, new kid, catch!" yelled Jason, the biggest and loudest of the boys, who was holding a football.

The ball hit Liam squarely on the face and made his nose bleed, but the big boy just laughed.

"You need to learn how to catch a ball!" he announced, loud enough for everyone to hear him.

Liam's eyes watered from the blow, but more so from the tears he was holding back. It was what he'd been afraid of all along – even at his old school he had been teased for not being interested in sport. But at least he'd had friends there. The same thing was happening now, except this time he was alone.

After getting some tissues, Liam looked around for Cara and Sophie in the playground, but there was no sign of them. Then he remembered Cara had said they would be at some kind of rehearsal for a musical.

He looked around for the music room but he couldn't see it, and he would never be able to hear music over the noise of the playground.

So, he did the next best thing – he followed the girl carrying the violin case.

Chapter 3

Georgia

Georgia hurried across the playground. She had left her sheet music in the music room. Looking in every direction, she made sure the mean girls were nowhere in sight to hold her up. She knew that they, particularly Zoe, might try to make her late for the audition.

She called them the "mean girls" in her head because that's what they were – mean.

Ever since Year Two, when Georgia had been big for her age, the teasing was relentless. And Zoe was the worst. She'd been her best friend once, but then Abby and Ella came along, and the three of them became the "cool" girls.

Georgia knocked on the music room door, and when nobody answered, she entered.

"Oh, it's you again, Georgia," said Miss Golding, surprised. "Sorry, I had my headphones on and didn't hear you knock. You didn't change your mind, did you?"

"No, Miss Golding. I am on my way to the performance hall now. I just forgot my sheet music," replied Georgia, feeling breathless.

Georgia was nervous. She could hardly believe that only minutes ago her music teacher had convinced her to audition for the school musical.

"We need a good orchestra," Miss Golding had told her, "and even more importantly, we need a good soloist. You'd be great for that, Georgia. Your clarinet and violin are the perfect instruments for *Aladdin*!"

It wasn't something Georgia had ever really thought about before. Being in front of people. Performing. She had stage fright – especially since the mean girls had made fun of her a couple of years ago, when she'd been on stage for the end-of-year concert.

They were nice to her when others were around, but when they found her alone at the lockers or the playground, they would make nasty comments about her music or make hurtful jokes that they thought were funny.

At first, Georgia had refused to put her name down for the orchestra audition. "I can't, Miss Golding. I'm too nervous, you know. I'm not a good performer."

But Miss Golding wouldn't take "no" for an answer. "You can't spend all your time just practising, Georgia. Don't you want other people to hear your beautiful music?"

"Yes, but …" Georgia hesitated. She didn't want to tell Miss Golding about Zoe and the others.

Georgia's parents had complained a number of times and the school always gave the mean girls warnings, but they would then tease Georgia in ways that were only obvious to Georgia.

There's no point in telling Miss Golding about it, thought Georgia, sadly. *She already knows about the mean girls.*

Miss Golding held up her hands. "Georgia, I know all about your situation. We all do at this school, and we want to help you, too. Those girls will not get away with bullying you or anyone else. We just need to make sure it is reported as soon as it happens. In the meantime, don't let them take away the one thing you really love – your music."

Georgia smiled for the first time in a long time. Miss Golding was right.

"Don't let them win, Georgia. You can do this. Show them and everyone else just how good you are!"

Still terrified, but excited, at the idea of performing in front of the school, Georgia had forgotten her sheet music. She knew the music off by heart, but it was her nerves that would let her down. She forgot everything when she was nervous.

She said goodbye to Miss Golding, and with the sheet music under her arm and her violin and clarinet in their cases, Georgia ran across the playground, careful not to catch the attention of the mean girls, and headed towards the hall.

She hadn't noticed the shadow behind her until she'd reached the steps. "Are you following me? Who are you?" she asked, not sure who the boy holding a tissue to his nose was.

"Sorry, I didn't mean to scare you," said Liam. "I'm new here and I'm looking for the music room. I thought since you had the violin case ..."

"Do you play an instrument, too?"

"Oh, no, I don't play anything. I was looking for Cara and Sophie. Do you know them? They're in my class and they said they were practising music or something today."

"Yes, I know them. They were in my class last year. I'm in 6C. And this is the hall, not the music room. But you won't find them in the music room anyway, because Miss Golding is coming over here to the hall now to start auditions for our end-of-year musical."

"Oh, so Cara and Sophie must be auditioning for the musical," said Liam.

"Maybe Cara is auditioning, but not Sophie. She doesn't like to speak in front of people," Georgia told him.

"So, what's the musical?" Liam wanted to know.

"*Aladdin,*" replied Georgia. "And I'm hoping to play in the orchestra."

"That sounds like fun," said Liam, sadly. "I used to love singing and dancing at my old school."

"Why don't you come in and see if there's something you'd like to audition for?" suggested Georgia. She'd never met a boy who liked to dance. At least, she didn't think she had.

"Well, I'm not sure …" Liam began. He didn't want to risk being bullied by the big boy, Jason, or the other boys at the school.

"Are you okay? Your face is dirty," said Georgia, staring at Liam's nose.

"I just got a blood nose," Liam replied. Then he added, "I, um … I get blood noses."

Liam thought it was best to lie, in case Jason found out he'd told someone about the football incident. *Best play it safe for now*, he thought.

"Come on. You may as well come inside the hall, where you can sit down and it's not so hot," said Georgia.

Chapter 4

Auditions

Sophie was the first to see Liam and Georgia walk into the hall. Cara was queuing up to go on stage, ready to sing.

Sophie waved. She felt sorry for Liam, being new at the school and not knowing anyone.

“Hi, Sophie,” said Liam, finding a seat next to her. “Is Cara auditioning now?”

She nodded.

“I met Georgia on the way. She’s going to try out for the orchestra,” Liam told her.

Sophie was surprised. She knew that Georgia hated being teased by the mean girls if she ever did anything to stand out. And being on stage was definitely standing out. She was glad she had said “no” when Cara begged her to try out for the singing part.

“You’ll be brilliant, Sophie. You know you can sing better than me. Better than anyone I know,” Cara had said.

"No way, Cara. You know how bad it will be if I stutter. Everyone will hate it – especially me. I'd want the ground to swallow me up and make me disappear. Forever!"

"But you know when you sing you don't stutter," Cara had insisted. She'd heard Sophie sing in the car, in the shower, in the backyard – Sophie loved singing, and never once did she stutter.

"That's because I don't sing in front of people," replied Sophie, annoyed. "Stop asking me. I don't want to do this. You do it."

In the end, Cara had given up asking her.

"Do you do err … s-s-sing or act?" Sophie asked Liam.

Liam hesitated for a few seconds. Now he understood why Sophie didn't speak up.

"Yes, I stutter," said Sophie. "It's better that you know now, and if you don't want to hang out with me, that's fine, just please don't tease me about it."

"I wouldn't tease you, Sophie. I know what it's like to be different. Yeah, I can sing, dance and act. Mostly, I love to dance, but I can do the other stuff, too," Liam replied.

"Really?" Sophie was interested.

"Yes," explained Liam. "At my old school there weren't many dancing classes – I came from a country town. All we had was ballroom dancing. So, I used to learn ballroom, and sometimes I'd get up and sing, too."

Sophie tried not to look shocked. She'd never met a boy who could dance, sing or act. All the boys she knew liked either sport or computers. But, then again, maybe some of them just pretended to like those things, because they thought they were supposed to.

"See, I'm not that different from you," said Liam. "We're just unique. What about you? Do you sing or dance?" asked Liam.

"I s-s-sing at home. That's as far as I will ever go," replied Sophie. "But Cara can sing, too, and she's up there on the stage. Shh … here she goes."

Cara's voice floated through the hall – it was strong, in tune and confident.

Miss Golding and the music director from the local theatre, Mr Joy, looked very happy. They were choosing the best performers for the roles in *Aladdin*. Their enthusiastic applause could only mean one thing: Cara was going to get the part.

"Hey, they just told me I got the part of Princess Jasmine!" said Cara, excitedly, when she returned to her seat.

"You were the best!" said Liam.

"Nah. Sophie can sing better than me," responded Cara. "I can't hold those really high notes, but I don't know anyone else who can either – except for Sophie."

"Look, Georgia's going up now," said Liam, pointing to the stage.

Georgia's nerves were making her shiver. She felt hot and clammy and then cold. She could see Liam, Sophie and Cara wave. That made her feel better.

Miss Golding smiled at her reassuringly. "Start with the clarinet, Georgia, and then we'll listen to your violin."

Georgia took a deep breath. Then she wet her lips, getting ready to blow into the clarinet. She kept her eyes on the music on the stand, so she wouldn't get distracted or nervous.

At the end of the piece, Miss Golding and Mr Joy gave an excited round of applause.

"Well done, Georgia. You can play the clarinet in the orchestra."

Georgia felt a rush of relief. Then, out of the corner of her eye she thought she saw Zoe, but Miss Golding had started speaking.

"Sorry, Miss Golding, I didn't hear what you said," Georgia said apologetically, her attention now back to her teacher.

"We'd like you to audition for the violin solo," Miss Golding told her. "We know you can play well enough for the orchestra, but we need a soloist and we think you'll be perfect."

Georgia gulped. She hated being the centre of attention. Performing a solo meant just that – playing the violin on her own. What if she forgot the notes? What if her fingers froze? What if …

"Georgia, please begin," said Miss Golding.

Georgia didn't take her eyes off the music sheet. She had played this piece over and over in her music lessons and at home. It was her favourite and when she played it, she imagined she was on a movie set with Princess Jasmine and Aladdin.

There was silence when she finished. Georgia's heart missed a beat. Was she that bad?

Miss Golding stood up and clapped very loudly. Then Mr Joy and everyone else who was watching joined in.

"You've definitely got the solo part, Georgia. Congratulations," announced Miss Golding, with a proud smile.

Georgia felt excited. She had done it! She glanced at all the other faces in the audience. Liam, Cara and Sophie were jumping up and down and waving. The only ones sitting down were Zoe, Abby and Ella. Zoe was holding her violin. She didn't look happy. In fact, she was glaring at Georgia.

It was clear to Georgia then that life was going to get more difficult for her. Zoe must have wanted the solo part. Now that Georgia had it, Zoe was going to make life miserable for her.

Georgia wished she had never auditioned for the solo.

Chapter 5

An Unexpected Try-out

"We need a boy to audition for Aladdin," called out Mr Joy. "Are there any boys here who want to come up now?"

Everyone in the hall went quiet. There were a few boys who were auditioning for fun roles of the genie and the thieves, but you didn't really need to sing or dance for those parts. The person who played Aladdin had to be good at singing, dancing and acting.

"Put your hand up, Liam," encouraged Sophie. "You told me you can dance, sing and act."

Liam stared straight ahead. He didn't know what to do. Part of him was excited to get a chance to do what he loved best. The other part of him was nervous and scared of what the other boys would think. Especially Jason. Liam was sick of being bullied.

Before Liam could decide, Cara quickly grabbed his arm and put it up. "Here's a volunteer, Mr Joy!"

All eyes were on Liam. “Come on up,” Mr Joy called out. “What’s your name, young man?”

“It’s Liam,” called out Cara.

“Maybe Liam can answer for himself,” Miss Golding laughed.

Liam cautiously walked to the stage. His knees were stiff, his heart was pounding and his mouth was dry. He wouldn’t be able to get any words out, he was sure.

“Show us what you can do,” said Mr Joy.

Liam wasn’t about to show them his ballroom dancing. It wasn’t that kind of dancing they wanted to see. He closed his eyes for a minute and remembered the steps he’d practised.

Liam had practised dancing after watching dance shows on television. He'd record them, and every day he'd go over and over the steps until he knew the routine was perfect.

He did all the dance steps exactly as he remembered them. It felt wonderful. Before he had a chance to stop, he heard Mr Joy call out, "Don't stop, sing as you dance!"

Liam sang a song from the movie *Aladdin* – he only knew the chorus, but he sang it over and over while he danced.

"Liam, can you now pretend that you are running away and jumping on all the roofs to make your escape?" he heard Miss Golding say.

He didn't have a chance to get nervous – Liam was pretending to leap over roofs, looking behind for the sultan's men chasing him and then giving a cheeky wave at the end before landing on the ground with a squat.

"What was that for?" asked Mr Joy.

"That was my camel waiting for me," replied Liam, with a cheeky grin.

"That was amazing!" someone called out.

"Excellent! We've found our Aladdin!"

"Bravo!"

Liam couldn't wait to get home. When his mum and dad would ask him what he did on his first day of school, he would be able to answer: "I got the lead role in the end-of-year production!"

"Looks like we're going to be spending a lot of time together at lunchtimes and after school for rehearsals," said Cara.

Georgia was quiet. She looked worried.

"That means you too, Georgia," added Sophie.

Cara nodded. "The four musketeers. That's us."

"See you all tomorrow for rehearsal," called out Miss Golding.

Georgia was relieved to have three new friends – it might keep Zoe and the mean girls away. It would be harder to tease four of them all at once, and she knew Cara would be loud enough to take attention away from Georgia.

Liam had made friends on his first day at the new school. He planned on making more friends. Except Jason – Liam had a feeling Jason was not going to like him. Ever. As long as Liam kept out of his way, everything was going to be fine.

Sophie was thrilled for her twin to have the singing part. It was perfect for Cara. She was outgoing and confident, whereas Sophie was the exact opposite. Only there was one thing that Sophie liked more than anything in the world – singing. Sadly, she'd never sing in front of people.

Her dream was never going to come true – even though it had felt so real!

Chapter 6

The Announcement

When the roles for the play were read out at next morning's school assembly, there were murmurs and stares. The first to be announced was the part of Aladdin. Most students were surprised to hear that Liam had the lead role, since he was so new. It was the first time most of the school had seen him.

Jason laughed out loud. It wasn't a friendly laugh. Liam's stomach tightened. He would have to be careful not to be anywhere near Jason alone.

Next to be read out was the part of Princess Jasmine. Cara was known as the friendliest girl in the school, so nearly everyone agreed that Cara was perfect for the part. Except for Abby, who had auditioned because she really wanted to become a celebrity one day.

Abby shot Cara a venomous glare. But Cara shrugged it off. She didn't care, as long as they didn't upset Sophie. It was Abby who had given Sophie the name, "Sophie the Stutterer".

When the principal, Mrs Hill, read out Georgia's name as the soloist, there was chattering among the students. Most of the Year 6 students didn't even know Georgia could play the violin – it had always been Zoe who had played the violin in all the school performances.

Everyone was looking at Zoe, who had an angry expression on her face. Georgia gulped. *Zoe is now officially the enemy*, Georgia thought.

"Students, we have a surprise guest coming to our production," Mrs Hill announced. "Our guest was once a student here, and she's coming to support our school and to help us raise funds for our new gym. She's looking forward to seeing our performance of *Aladdin*."

Everyone held their breath. This was a complete surprise.

"The name of our special guest is Katie West."

Abby, Ella and Zoe squealed so loudly that everyone jumped in fright. Katie West was a singer who had won *I Can Sing*, a talent show on television. She was now the most popular singer in the country, and her new single was a number-one hit around the world.

That's a lucky break, thought Georgia. Hopefully, Zoe and her friends would now concentrate on trying to meet Katie West, and would forget about Georgia's solo.

The other good thing was that with the four of them walking together to the hall at lunchtime for the rehearsal, and with Miss Golding close by, any kind of meeting with the bullies was avoided. All Zoe, Abby and Ella could do was glare from a distance. For now.

For the first week of rehearsals, it seemed that the four musketeers were left alone. There were no nasty encounters with the mean girls or Jason. Each day at lunchtime and twice a week after school, the four friends would meet at the hall and have a great time rehearsing. Even Sophie, who wasn’t in the show itself, had a job to do, helping with costumes and changing sets.

But all that was about to change. It all started when Cara developed a bad cough.

Chapter 7

Some Unfortunate Events

"You'll have to go to school without me, Sophie. I'm sick," moaned Cara.

"But we always go to school together. If you're staying home, then I'm staying home," insisted Sophie.

Sophie was scared to go to school without her sister. Cara was the one who did the talking for her, the one who looked out for her and kept the mean girls away. There was no way she was going to go to school without her.

"Sophie, you have to go to school. The doctor says that Cara needs to stay home for a few days. You can't stay home if you're not sick," said their mum.

"Then I'll catch a cold, too," replied Sophie, angrily.

"What about Liam and Georgia? They need you there, Sophie," said Cara. "You can be the three musketeers while I'm away."

"You'll be fine on your own, Sophie. You've made some good friends," said Mum.

But Sophie had a horrible feeling about it all. She felt sick at the thought of being without Cara.

As soon as Sophie walked on her own through the school gates, Abby, Ella and Zoe appeared.

"St-st-stuttering Sophie. Where's your other half?" Zoe sniggered.

"You were conjoined twins, right? You know, had to be separated at birth? Well, that's what I heard," Abby said nastily.

"Oh, by the way, I've just taken a photo of you on my phone. Never know what I could do with it ..." Ella chimed in.

The three of them smirked and giggled in a way that made Sophie frightened and angry at the same time. Cara would have known what to say. Instead, Sophie just froze.

She was about to turn back and hide somewhere out on the basketball court, when she heard Liam shout, "Leave her alone!" Then, he ran over, making weird noises and jumping around to bring attention to him.

"He's seriously weird," said Abby. "Let's leave these two alone."

The three girls turned their backs and walked towards class, laughing together.

"Are you okay?" asked Liam, when they'd gone.

Sophie was shaking and pale. "I don't know why they took my photo. I'm worried."

"It'll be all right. We'll tell Mrs Hill," he replied.

"It'll be too late by then," said Sophie, shakily. "Abby is awful. Sh-sh-she's furious that she didn't get the main part in the show, and she's going to make me suffer now that Cara's not here to defend me."

"Come on, let's go to class. I'll find Georgia and we'll stick with you all day," said Liam.

Liam was worried about Sophie. He knew what it felt like to be scared and alone.

By the end of the day, Sophie's photo had been sent to everyone in Year 6, with the message:

Sophie wanted to cry. She felt so embarrassed. Some of her classmates felt sorry for her, but no one did anything to make her feel better.

It was bad enough that Sophie was humiliated, but the mean girls weren't going to forget about Georgia, either. They were furious that Georgia had been given the solo part instead of Zoe.

"You're just a teacher's pet," Zoe said to Georgia angrily after school. "You know I'm a better violinist than you. I've always been better than you. I played the violin before you did. You've always copied me."

Georgia took a deep breath and tried to remain calm. *Sticks and stones can break my bones, but words can never hurt me*, she said, over and over in her head.

But in her heart, the words did hurt her.

That same afternoon, Liam was doing laps of the oval near his house. He enjoyed running; it helped keep him fit for dancing. He didn't realise the oval was used for football practice – Jason's football practice – until it was too late.

"What are *you* doing here?" Jason called out loudly, approaching him, a football in his hand.

There were only a few other boys playing on the oval, and they didn't seem interested in playing with Jason. The only adults around were on the far side of the oval and they couldn't see what was going on. If Jason decided to throw the football at Liam's nose again, there would be nobody there to see it.

Think, Liam, think hard, he thought to himself.

"I came here to practise," Liam said, once he found his voice.

Jason scoffed. "What? You, practise? You don't play footy, or any sport."

"Throw the ball and I'll show you how good I am," said Liam, keeping his fingers crossed that he could buy some time before the coach and the other players arrived.

Confused, Jason threw the ball over to Liam. It went over Liam's head. Liam ran to pick it up.

"You can't even catch a pass!" teased Jason.

"Well, you can't catch me!" replied Liam, and he picked up the football and ran.

Liam could see Jason chasing him, but Liam was a fast runner. He could have been in the athletics team if he wanted to, but Liam wanted to dance instead.

Jason did his best to catch up to Liam, but Liam was too fast. When he got close, Liam would dodge and leap and run in a different direction. Jason was soon out of breath. His breathing became hard and he lay on the grass, panting and gasping for air.

Liam stopped running. He could have stopped earlier or even run to where he could see the coach training the other boys in the football team. But he had wanted to show Jason that he was a good runner, and not just a dancer. Running wasn't a team sport like football, but it was still a sport.

Liam jogged back to where Jason was lying, and he left the ball on the ground. “Have a great game.”

He saw Jason stare at him, his mouth open. Nobody had ever done that to Jason before – beaten him at anything. Liam hoped there wasn’t going to be any trouble tomorrow at school. What if Jason cornered him at lunchtime? He’d have to make sure he stayed near a teacher all the time. Maybe he could stay in the first-aid room and say he was sick.

Chapter 8

A Special Request

Cara's cold had turned into a serious chest infection and then bronchitis. Her voice was sounding terrible and her throat hurt whenever she tried to sing.

"Sophie, you have to sing for me. The production is next week. My voice isn't strong enough to sing," Cara begged. "Please do this for me. I know you have a beautiful voice, and I don't want Abby to take my place. You know how much she wants my role. We can't let her get what she wants!"

But nothing Cara said would make Sophie change her mind.

"I can be on stage doing the acting, as long as you sing," continued Cara. "You don't even have to be on stage. I'll just move my lips. Everyone will think it's me singing."

"No!" said Sophie. "I'll just stutter, and then the performance will be ruined."

No one was more surprised than Sophie when she was called to the principal's office. It was the first time ever in her six years at the school. But she was even more surprised when she saw who else was there. Why did Mrs Hill want to talk to her with Zoe, Abby and Ella?

"I've asked you all to come here because I have received an email from Katie West," began Mrs Hill. "She says she's looking forward to the performance next week."

Abby's face flushed. She was so excited at the thought of meeting Katie West. Zoe and Ella looked just as excited.

"However," said Mrs Hill, in a serious voice, "I have decided that only Sophie will be meeting Katie West."

There was a stunned silence in the room.

"Sophie, Katie West has requested to meet you, specifically."

Abby, Zoe and Ella glared at Sophie.

"You see," Mrs Hill explained, "it seems that Katie stuttered when she was at school, so she wants to give you, Sophie, some words of confidence and encouragement."

Sophie stared in shock at Mrs Hill.

"As for you, Abby," continued Mrs Hill, "I have heard reports that you have been teasing Sophie. Because of this, I've decided that you will not be invited to the production."

Abby blushed a deep red, and for once it seemed like she was at a loss for something to say. "But – but it's not only me …" she stammered, looking at her two friends.

"Oh, yes, we are well aware of your friends," said Mrs Hill. "Zoe and Ella, you will also not be welcome at the production."

Zoe and Ella squirmed. They were too shocked and upset to say anything.

"Zoe, Miss Golding has told me that you've been very unkind to a student who is extremely talented at playing the violin. I wouldn't like to think that perhaps you are jealous," continued Mrs Hill.

Zoe's face went red. She was embarrassed and ashamed that Mrs Hill thought she was jealous.

"I suggest that if all three of you make an effort to improve the situation, then perhaps I might change my mind on the matter," Mrs Hill finished, and she opened the door for them to leave.

Alone with Mrs Hill, Sophie remained frozen on the spot. She didn't know what to say.

"Your mother came to see me," Mrs Hill explained. "Cara told her what you and your friends have been going through. We are going to do our best to help you. Now, you need to help us, Sophie. We need someone to sing Cara's part. I will not allow Abby to participate, but it will be disappointing for the whole production team if we are missing our lead singer. Will you do it?"

Sophie nodded. "Yes, Mrs Hill. I'll do my best."

She didn't know how she was going to sing in front of so many people, but she'd give it a try. The show must go on.

When Sophie met up with Georgia and Liam, they could hardly believe their luck.

"That explains why Zoe was so friendly to me today," said Georgia. "But she did say something really strange …"

"What?" said Sophie and Liam at the same time.

Georgia frowned, looking confused. "She told me to 'break a leg'!"

"Why would she say that? That's awful!" said Sophie.

"No, in show business, 'break a leg' means 'good luck'," explained Liam.

The mean girls had to be friendly and polite to everyone at the school, but especially to Sophie and Georgia. Without the fear of running into them and being teased, Georgia could concentrate on learning her solo.

Georgia smiled, and suddenly felt more confident than ever before.

"What about Jason?" Georgia asked Liam. "Aren't you worried that he's going to do something to you?"

"Mrs Hill has put him in charge of changing the sets, and curtain opening and closing. I think he has to behave. And so far, he's left me alone," replied Liam.

"Are you nervous?" Sophie asked her two friends.

"Totally nervous!" they replied at the same time.

"But we'll do it anyway, because nerves mean that you want to do well and that you care about your performance," added Liam.

"Don't worry, Sophie, everything is going to go well!" said Georgia.

But Sophie did worry. She worried a lot.
She wished she could catch a bad cold, too.

Chapter 9

Break a Leg!

The opening night of the musical had finally arrived. The four friends held hands in a circle backstage.

"Break a leg!" they whispered to each other.

People began to fill the rows. Parents, students, teachers and other guests sat in their seats, chatting excitedly to each other.

After Zoe, Abby and Ella's good behaviour, they had been allowed to come to the production after all. They sat with their parents in the back row. Mrs Hill walked down the aisle and smiled at everyone, making sure everybody was seated and ready for the performance.

Liam practised his jumps and turns on stage, behind the closed curtains. On one of his turns, he saw that Jason was watching him from the side of the stage.

"Are you sure you don't want to play footy?" Jason asked him. "You're a good runner."

Liam shook his head. "Nah. I prefer dancing any day. But thanks for the offer," he said, with a grin.

For the first time, he now felt truly ready to go out on stage.

Georgia took a deep breath as she finished tuning her violin. Her clarinet was next to her on its stand. She was as ready as she would ever be to face her stage fright.

Sophie's stomach was churning with nerves. Her chest hurt. She felt like she couldn't breathe. *What if I stutter?* she thought.

"You'll be fine," said a voice coming from behind the curtains. "If I could do it, so can you."

Sophie looked at Katie West and smiled. It meant so much to Sophie to hear her say that. Katie was someone she wanted to be like. She was brave and did her very best to achieve her dream.

If only I could be like her and have my dream come true, thought Sophie, as she remembered her dream of a perfect singing performance.

She was ready at last.

The noise from the audience got louder as Katie appeared from backstage and sat in the front row.

"Places, everybody," whispered Miss Golding. "Let the show begin!"

The audience was amazed. They kept clapping for ages after the curtain came down. There were repeated calls of:

"Bravo!"

"More!"

"Well done!"

During the performance there had been "oohs" and "ahhs" and laughs in all the right places, but nobody had expected the wild reaction from the audience when Sophie started to sing.

Sophie had not stuttered once. She hadn't even hesitated.

The audience gasped as they heard Sophie reach the highest notes in perfect tune, while Cara acted the part of Princess Jasmine.

It was a brilliant combination of a beautiful voice with talented acting. Sophie's dream really had come true.

After the third curtain call, Katie West came onto the stage to make a speech.

“This has been the highest quality school production I’ve ever been to,” Katie addressed the excited audience. “You should all be very proud. The dancing and music were amazing. The acting was brilliant. But what impressed me most, and what you may not have realised, was that the part of Princess Jasmine was sung from backstage. Sophie, you should be very proud of your singing. Ladies and gentleman, can you please put your hands together and give Sophie a special round of applause? Sophie, please come out on stage and take a bow.”

Sophie felt very honoured to be singled out, but she knew how hard her sister and her friends had worked. When the curtain rose, Sophie grabbed Liam, Georgia and Cara and pulled them onto the stage with her.

They took a bow together.

The audience stood up and continued to clap and whistle.

The friends – the four musketeers – had managed to do what they thought was impossible: to perform in front of the school, their parents, and others, including the bullies.

"You did a wonderful job, all of you," said Mrs Hill, at the end of the evening.

"Thank you. I hope we will be able to keep performing together at our next school," replied Liam.

"Which school do you all want to go to?" Mrs Hill wanted to know.

"Well, I like the kind of school where there isn't any teasing or bullying, for starters," said Sophie.

"And a good music department," said Georgia.

"As well as drama and dancing," added Liam.

"Can you suggest a school that has all of these, Mrs Hill?" asked Cara.

Mrs Hill smiled. “I hear Pinehill High School has an excellent performing arts department. It sounds like a perfect fit for you all.”

The four friends looked at each other, and then hugged each other excitedly.

“Pinehill High School, here we come!” they called out. “The four musketeers, friends forever!”